Coldplay

••

Prospekt's Ma

Wise Publications
part of The Music Sales Group
London/New York/Paris/Sydney/Copenhagen/Berlin/Madrid/Tokyo

Published by
Wise Publications
14-15 Berners Street, London
W1T 3LJ, UK.

Exclusive distributors:
Music Sales Limited
Distribution Centre, Newmarket Road,
Bury St Edmunds, Suffolk
IP33 3YB, UK.

Music Sales Pty Limited
20 Resolution Drive, Caringbah
NSW 2229, Australia.

Order No. AM996688
ISBN 978-1-84772-958-3

Music arranged by Derek Jones and Jack Long.
Music processed by Paul Ewers Music Design.
Edited by Jenni Wheeler.

Cover painting by Eugéne Delacroix.
Original CD design by Tappin Gofton.
Photography by Stephan Crasneanscki.

Printed in the EU.

Life In Technicolor ii

Words & Music by
Guy Berryman, Chris Martin, Jon Buckland, Will Champion & Jon Hopkins

A/E
A
A
F♯m7
Dmaj7
A
Esus4
A
There's a wild_

A
wind blow - ing down the cor - ner of my street;
ev - 'ry night there the head - lights are glow -
F#m7
Dmaj7
- ing. There's a cold war com - ing, on the ra -
A
Esus4
- di - o I heard. Ba - by, it's a

A
vi - 'lent world.
Oh,
F♯m D A/C♯
love, don't let me go.
Won't you take
F♯m D A/C♯
me where the street lights glow?
I can hear
F♯m D A A/G♯ F♯m7
it com - ing,
I can hear the si - ren's sound;
like a se - re - nade of sound;
now my

Esus4
To Coda ⊕
A
feet won't touch the ground.
F♯m
D
A
F♯m
D
A
Time
F♯m
D
A
came a-creep-ing, oh, and time's a load-ed gun. Ev-'ry road

F♯m
D
A/C♯
is a ray of light. It goes
F♯m
D
A
on, time on-ly can lead you on. Still it's
Esus4
A
D.S. al Coda
such a beau - ti-ful night. Oh.
Coda
A
F♯m
D

A/C♯ F♯m D
A/C♯ F♯m D
Grav - i - ty re - lease me, and don't ev -
A A/G♯ F♯m7 Esus4
- er hold me down, now my feet won't touch
A
the ground.

Postcards From Far Away

Words & Music by
Guy Berryman, Chris Martin, Jon Buckland & Will Champion

Glass Of Water

Words & Music by
Guy Berryman, Chris Martin, Jon Buckland & Will Champion

A7sus4/D A/D D A7sus4/D A/D
- ter, the rip - ples and the lines. And he asked
Dsus4 Asus4
"Will I see heav-en in mine?"
D A7sus4/D A/D D A7sus4/D A/D D
2. That
A7sus4/D A/D D A7sus4/D A/D D
is just the way it was. Noth - ing could be
(3.) he wrote it on a wall. The hol - low - est of

A7sus4/D A/D D A7sus4/D A/D D
bet-ter and noth - ing ev - er was. Oh, they
ha-los is no ha - lo at all. Tel-
A7sus4/D A/D D A7sus4/D A/D D
say you can see your fu - ture in-side a glass of wa-
- e - vi - sion sell - ing plas - tic fi - gures of lead-
A7sus4/D A/D D A7sus4/D A/D
- ter, the rid - dles and the rhymes.
- ers say-ing noth - ing at all. And you chime
Dsus4 A Asus4
Will I see heav-en in mine?
"Stars in heav-en a - lign."
Oh, ah.

D F♯m Bm7 G/D
Son, don't
D F♯m Bm7 G/D
ask. Nei - ther
D F♯m Bm7 G/D
half full or emp - ty is your
D F♯m Bm7 G/D D
glass. Cling

F♯m
Bm7
G/D
D
F♯m
to the mast.
Bm7
G/D
D
F♯m
Bm7
Spend your whole life living
G
Gmaj9
D/E
Gmaj9
Asus4
To Coda
in the past.
Going nowhere fast.
D
A7sus4/D
A/D
D
A7sus4/D
A/D
3fr

D
A7sus4/D
A/D
D
A7sus4/D
A/D
D.S. al Coda
3. So
Coda
Gsus♯4
A7/G
8vb
F♯m7
Bm
(8)
G7
Em7
(8)

Asus4
A
(8)
D
F#m
Bm7
Gadd9/D
D
F#m
Bm7
Gadd9/D
D
D
A
Oh, what are we drink-ing when we're done?
G
D
Glass-es of wa - ter.

Rainy Day

Words & Music by
Guy Berryman, Chris Martin, Jon Buckland & Will Champion

E♭ A♭ D♭ E♭ A♭ D♭
rain. The sky wore a veil of gold and green. At night it was the bright of the moon
rain. I spent the night with the Queen of Spain. My lone-ly lit-tle heart would have broke
E♭ A♭ D♭ E♭
with me. Time is just float-ing.
a-gain. Time is so vi-cious.
A♭ D♭ E♭ A♭ D♭
Then there was rain. The sound foun-da-tions are crum-
The deep-er that the knife goes in the more you win.
E♭ A♭ D♭ E♭
bl-ing. Through the ground comes a bit of a tum-bl-ing. And time
You end up with less than when you be-gin. The deep-er that the knife goes in.

A♭ D♭ E♭ A♭ D♭
4fr 4fr 6fr 4fr 4fr
was just float-ing a-way. We can watch it and stay and we can lis-ten.
Oh.
1° only
E♭
6fr
D♭ A♭ E♭
4fr 4fr 6fr
Oh, rain-y day come a-round.
D♭maj7 A♭ E♭
4fr 4fr 6fr
Some-times I just want it to slow down.

D♭maj7
Fm7
E♭
We're sep - a - rat - ed now, I'm down. But I love
D♭maj7
A♭
E♭
1.
when you come o-ver to my house. I love it when you come o-ver to my house.
2.
E♭
D♭maj7
A♭
E♭
Oh.

D♭maj7
A♭
E♭
Oh.
D♭maj7
Fm7
E♭
Oh.
D♭maj7
A♭
E♭
And I love it when you come o-ver to my house. I love it when you come o-ver to my house.
D♭maj7
A♭
E♭
I love it when you come o-ver to my house. I love it when you come o-ver to my house.

Prospekt's March / Poppyfields

Words & Music by
Guy Berryman, Chris Martin, Jon Buckland & Will Champion

Bm
A/C♯
G
speak - ing.
Try'n - a take what they can get.
Bm
A/C♯
G
Bm
I ask you if you re - mem - ber.
E7
Gadd9
2fr
Pros - pekt how could I for - get?
Drums,
D
Bm7
here it comes.

G
Don't you wish that life could be as sim - ple as fish
E7
swim - ming 'round in a bar - rel when you've got the gun?
Gm
D
Oh, and I run.
Here it comes.
Bm7
We're just two

G
lit-tle fi-gures in a soup bowl, try'n-a get the oth-er kind-a con-trol. But I
Em
Gadd9
2fr
was-n't one. But here I
A
F♯m7
Gmaj9
3
lie on my own in a sep-a-rate sky.
A
F♯m7
3
And here I lie on my own in a sep-a-rate

Gmaj9
A
sky.
I don't wan-na die
F♯m7
Gmaj9
on my own here to-night.
But here I
A
F♯m7
lie
on my own in a sep-a-rate
3
Gmaj9
Dadd9
2fr
sky.

Lost+

Words & Music by
Guy Berryman, Chris Martin, Jon Buckland, Will Champion & Shawn Carter

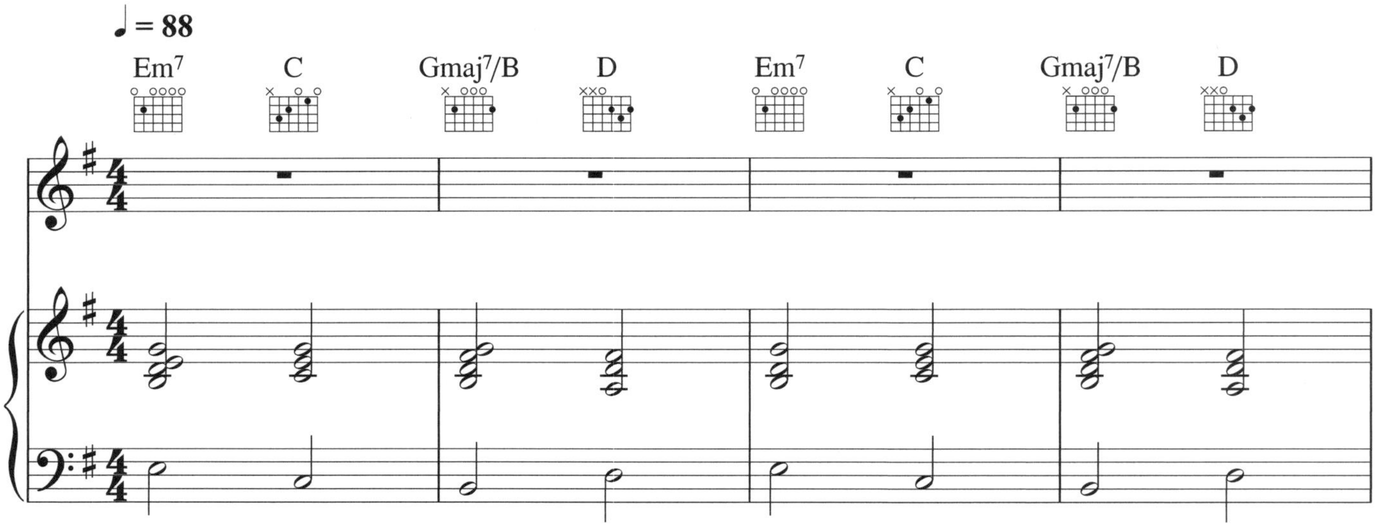

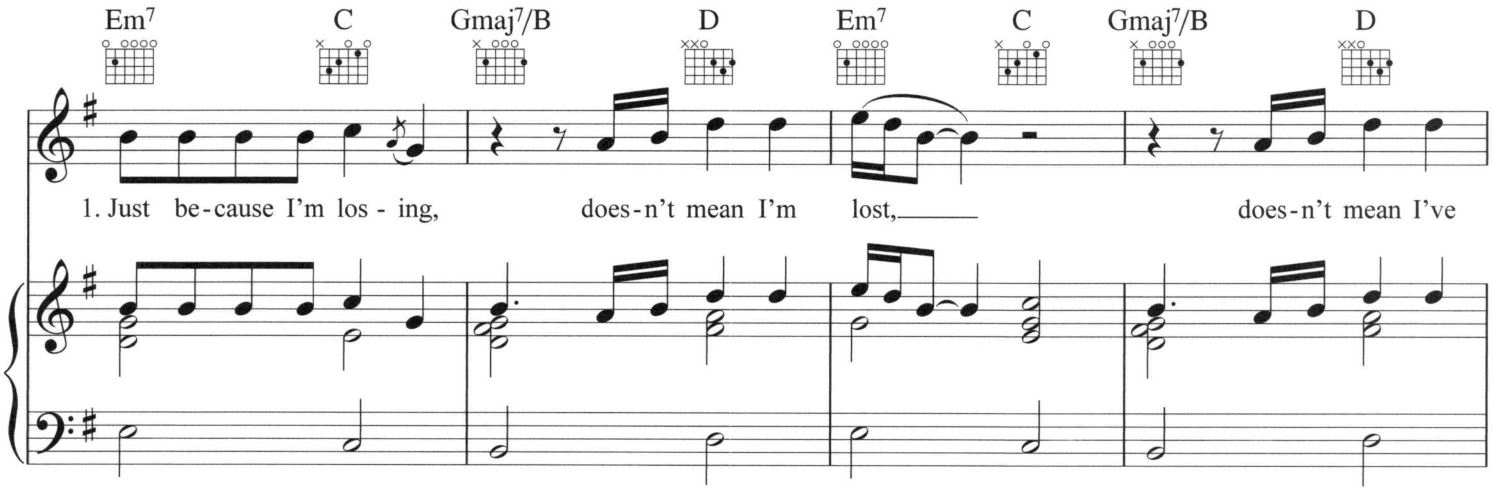

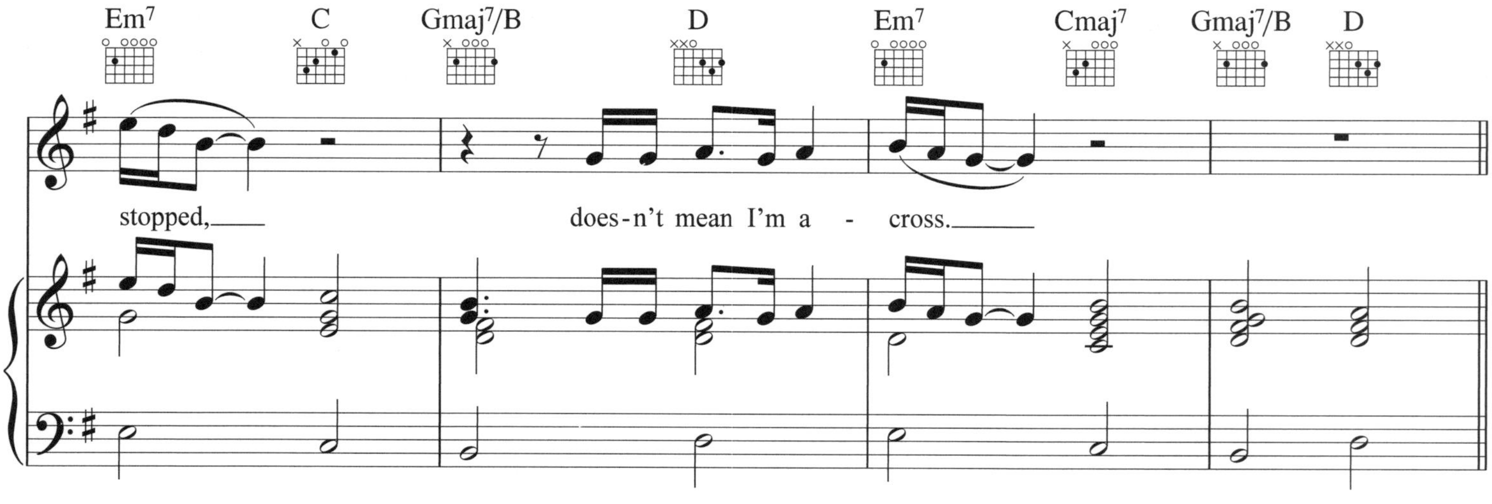

Em7 C Gmaj7/B D Em7 C
2. Just be - cause I'm hurt - ing, does - n't mean I'm hurt,
3. You might be a big fish in a lit - tle pond;
Gmaj7/B D Em7 C Gmaj7/B D
does - n't mean I did - n't get what I de - served; no bet - ter and no
does - n't mean you've won, 'cause a - long may come a big - ger
Em7 Cmaj7 Bm7 D
worse. I just got lost.
one. And you'll be lost.
C G D
Ev - 'ry riv - er that I tried to cross,
Ev - 'ry riv - er that you tried to cross,

C G D
ev - 'ry door I ev - er tried was locked. Oh, and I'm
ev - 'ry gun you ev - er held went off. Oh, and I'm
C G D
1.
just wait-ing till the shine wears off.
just wait-ing till the fir - ing's stopped.
2.
D C
Oh, and I'm just
G D
wait-ing till the shine wears off. (Spoken:) A - ha, I got-cha, uh... With the

Em7
C
Gmaj7/B
D
same sword they knight you, they gon' good-night you with, shit, that's on-ly half if they like you.
Em7
C
D
Bm
That ain't e-ven the half what they might do, don't be-lieve me, ask Mich-ael.
Em7
C
Gmaj7/B
D
See Mar-tin, see Mal-colm, see Big-gie, see Pac, see suc-cess and its out-come.
Em7
C
D
Bm
See Je-sus, see Ju-das, see Cae-sar, see Bru-tus. See, suc-cess is like su-i-cide.

Em C Bm D
Su - i - cide, it's a su - i - cide, if you suc - ceed, pre-pare to be cru - ci-fied.
Em C D Bm
Me-di-a med-dles, nig-gers sue you, you set-tle. Ev-'ry step you take, they re-mind you you're ghet-to.
Em C Bm D
So it's tough be-ing Bob - by Brown; to be Bob-by then, you have to be Bob - by now. And the
Em C D Bm
ques-tion is: is to have had and lost bet-ter than not hav-ing at all? Be- cause...
Oh, and I'm

C
G
just wait - ing till the shine wears off.
2° Instrumental
D
C
Oh, and I'm just
G
D
G/D
D
wait - ing till the shine wears off.
Em7
C
Gmaj7/B
D
Em7
C
Gmaj7/B
Repeat and fade

Lovers In Japan (Osaka Sun Mix)

Words & Music by
Guy Berryman, Chris Martin, Jon Buckland & Will Champion

G
G
D6
1. Lov - ers,
keep on the road you're on,
(2.) - night,
may-be we're gon - na run,
Cmaj7
run - ners
un - til the race is
dream - ing
of the O - sa - ka
G
run.
Sol - diers,
sun.
Oh.

D6
you've got to sol - dier on.
Oh.
Some -
Dream -
Cmaj7
3fr
G
- times e - ven the right is wrong.
- ing of when the morn - ing comes.
Em
C
G
They are turn - ing my head out to
D
Em
C
see what I'm all a - bout.
Keep - ing my head down

G
D
Em
to see what it feels like now. I
G/D
C
Am
have no doubt, one day we're
the
D
Em7
Cmaj7
1.
gon - na get out.
sun will come out.
G
D
G6

Cmaj7/G
G
D/G
2. To -
2.
Em
Cadd9
G/B
D
Em
Cadd9
G/B
D
D/A
Em/B

Cadd9
G/B
D
Em/B
Cadd9
G/B
D
G

Now My Feet Won't Touch The Ground

Words & Music by
Guy Berryman, Chris Martin, Jon Buckland & Will Champion

G
C
Rocks a - wait - ing boys, if rocks a -
F
Am
Em7
- wait, swoop down from the sky and catch
F
Gsus4
3fr
C
me like a bird of prey.
C
F
C
Now my feet won't touch the ground.

Gsus4
G
Now my head won't stop. You
C
wait a life - time to be found.
F
C
To Coda
Now my feet won't touch the ground.
C
F

C
Gsus4
G
C
F
Am7
Em
F
Gsus4
C
D.S. al Coda
Sing-ing
Coda
C
Fmaj7
G
C5
Now my feet won't touch the ground.

A Spell A Rebel Yell

Words & Music by
Guy Berryman, Chris Martin, Jon Buckland & Will Champion

C
Csus4
C
1. As far as I can see, all time and
Csus4
F/A
Gomit5/B
F/C
F
cir - cuit - ry is wrong.
Csus4
C
Csus4
C
Csus4
Csus4
C
Csus4
C
2. As far as po - et - ry, sit down and
3. Sol - dier, come home to me, you've been a -

Csus4
F/A
Gomit5/B
F/C
F
Csus4
C
sing to me a song.
-way from me so long.
Csus4
C
Csus4
'Cause all I
All I
want in this world, all I
C
Csus4
F/A
Gomit5/B
F/C
F
want in this world is for you to come home.
Csus4
C
Csus4
Csus4
C
1.
Csus4
A spell, a re - bel yell; a spell.

2.
Csus4
Csus4
C
A re - bel yell.
A spell,
Csus4
C
Csus4
a re - bel yell.
A spell,
a re - bel yell.
F/A
Gomit5/B
F/C
F
Csus4
C
Oh.
A spell,
Csus4
C
Csus4
Repeat and fade
a re - bel yell.
A spell,
a re - bel yell.

Death Will Never Conquer

Words & Music by
Guy Berryman, Chris Martin, Jon Buckland & Will Champion

B♭7 E♭ A♭ E♭ E♭
go boys, let me go.
2. One day death is gon-na
(3.) sweet death should ev-er
A♭ E♭ B♭7
con-quer me, I'll be down where the wa-ters flow. I hope
con-quer me, take me down to some place be-low. If you
To Coda
E♭ A♭6 E♭ B♭7 E♭
sweet Heav-en has a place for me. Let me know boys, let me know.
hear him com-ing, won't you set me free? Let me go boys, let me go.
A♭ E♭ E♭ A♭/E♭ E♭

B♭7/F
E♭
A♭/E♭
E♭
B♭/F
E♭
D.S. al Coda
3. If
Coda
A♭/E♭
E♭
Cm
E♭/B♭
If you hear him com - ing, won't you
A♭
E♭
B♭7
E♭
say for me, that I just don't want to go?

The Goldrush

Words & Music by
Guy Berryman, Chris Martin, Jon Buckland & Will Champion

Dm
B♭
F
told.
I'm march-ing through the cold.
I'm / we're march-ing through the cold.
1.
2, 3.
Dm
B♭
2. I
There's a ti - ny lit-tle crack-le on the tel-e-phone line.
F
Dm
B♭
Say-ing what use the met-al if the met-al don't shine?
F
Dm
B♭
She said bring me back a dia-mond 'cause I real-ly want one.

F
Dm
B♭
To Coda
I've been dig - ging so long that I nev - er see the
F
D.S. al Coda
sun.
3. I
Coda F
Dm
B♭
sun. I've been dig - ging so long that I nev - er see the
F
Dm
B♭
F
sun. I've been dig - ging so long that I nev - er see the sun.

Lhuna

Words & Music by
Guy Berryman, Chris Martin, Jon Buckland & Will Champion

Original key B♭ minor

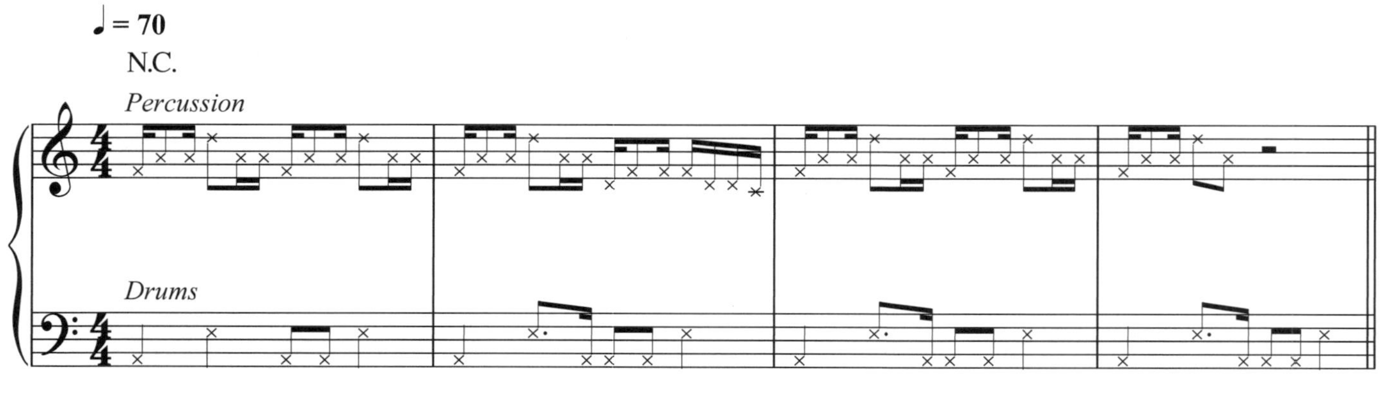

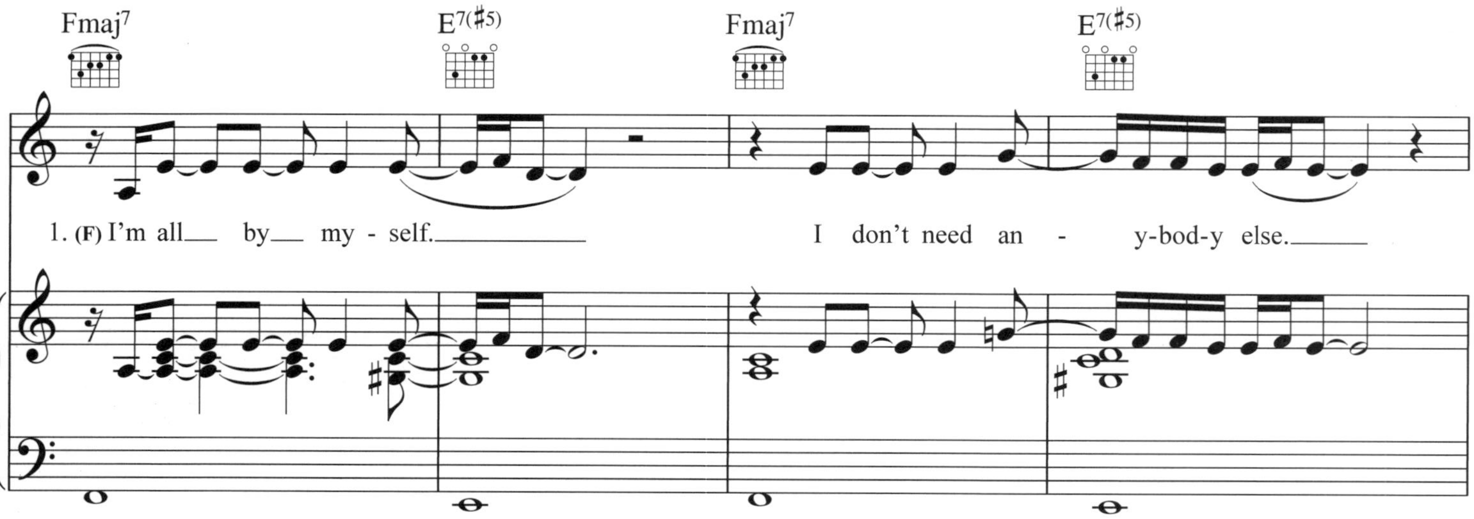

Fmaj7
E7(♯5)
Fmaj7
2. I'm all on my own. Quiet - ly sleep-
3. (F) I don't know what the time is. I don't know where you've
E7(♯5)
Fmaj7
E7(♯5)
- ing in my home. I'm all on my own. My own.
flown. And I don't know why you're so far from
Am/C
E7/B
Am
B♭7
home.
(M) Hel-lo, won't you let me come in?
Am6
A♭dim7
Am
Lhu-na, can't you hear how much I'm suf-fer-ing? Hel-lo, won't you

B♭7 F D
let me know? 'Cause I'm all a - lone. I'm all a - lone. (M/F) We are
Am C Dm
dream - ing a - bout Lhu - na. The smell of her,
B♭ Am C
the touch and the taste of her. Dream - ing a - bout Lhu - na. Her
Bdim7 1. E7 2. E7
and me si - mul - ta - neous - ly. - ta - neous - ly. Her

Dm
B♭7
Dm
B♭7
and me, ef-fort-less-ly. Oh, her and me, ef-fort-less-ly.
Am
C6
Dm
B♭
Am
C6
(F) Ooh. Ooh. Ooh. Ooh. Ooh.
Bdim7
E7(♯5)
Dm
B♭7
Dm
Ooh. Ah.
B♭7
Am
Am(add9)
Am
Ooh.

Lost?

Words & Music by
Guy Berryman, Chris Martin, Jon Buckland & Will Champion

Em C Gmaj7/B Dadd11 Em C
2. Just be-cause I'm hurt-ing, does-n't mean I'm hurt,
3. You might be a big fish in a lit-tle pond;
Gmaj7/B Dadd11 Em C Gmaj7/B Dadd11
does-n't mean I did-n't get what I de-served: no bet-ter and no
does-n't mean you've won, 'cause a-long may come a big-ger
Em C Gmaj7/B Dadd11 D
worse. I just got lost. Ev-'ry riv-er that I
one. And you'll be lost. Ev-'ry riv-er that you
C G D C G
tried to cross, ev-'ry door I ev-er tried was
tried to cross, ev-'ry gun you ev-er held went

D C G
locked. Oh, and I'm just wait-ing till the shine wears off.
off. Oh, and I'm just wait-ing till the fir - ing's stopped.
1. D
2. D
Oh, and I'm
C G D
just wait-ing till the shine wears off.
Em C D Bm Em C D Bm

Em C D Bm Em C D Bm
Oh, and I'm
C G/B D
just wait-ing till the shine wears off.
Oh, and I'm
C G D
just wait - ing till the shine wears off.
poco rit.
Em C Gmaj7/B Dadd11 Em

1 2 3 4 5 6 7 8 9

Classical Dances for Solo Piano

Fifteen celebrated classical dance pieces
by the world's greatest composers

Wise Publications
part of The Music Sales Group
London/New York/Paris/Sydney/Copenhagen/Berlin/Madrid/Tokyo

Published by

Wise Publications
14 – 15 Berners Street, London W1T 3LJ, UK

Exclusive Distributors:

Music Sales Limited
Distribution Centre, Newmarket Road, Bury St Edmunds, Suffolk IP33 3YB, UK.

Music Sales Corporation
257 Park Avenue South, New York, NY 10010, USA.

Music Sales Pty Limited
120 Rothschild Avenue, Rosebery, NSW 2018, Australia.

Order No. AM988746
ISBN 1-84609-852-1

Edited by Rachel Payne
Cover design by Chloë Alexander
Cover image Das Menuett / Kupferstich by J.E. Nilson courtesy of akg-images
Printed in the EU

Your Guarantee of Quality
As publishers, we strive to produce every book to the highest commercial standards.
This book has been carefully designed to minimise awkward page turns and to make playing from it a real pleasure.
Particular care has been given to specifying acid-free, neutral-sized paper made from pulps which have not been elemental chlorine bleached. This pulp is from farmed sustainable forests and was produced with special regard for the environment.
Throughout, the printing and binding have been planned to ensure a sturdy, attractive publication which should give years of enjoyment.
If your copy fails to meet our high standards, please inform us and we will gladly replace it.

www.musicsales.com

Bourée in G minor

Composed By George Frideric Handel

Dance Of The Hours

From 'La Gioconda'

Composed By Amilcare Ponchielli

Moderato (♩ = c.160)

'THE HOURS OF DAY'

10
Meno mosso (♩ = c.132)
'THE HOURS OF NIGHT'
espress.
14
18
22
rit.
a tempo
26

rall.
Allegro con brio (♪ = c.168)
'DANCE OF ALL THE HOURS'
1.
2.

Dance Of The Sugar Plum Fairy

From 'The Nutcracker'

Composed By Peter Ilyich Tchaikovsky

Andante non troppo

(8)
(8)
loco

mf
loco
ff
(8)
(8)
loco
f

GAVOTTE

FROM SUITE FOR ORCHESTRA IN D

COMPOSED BY JOHANN SEBASTIAN BACH

16
19
mf
23
27
31

35
f
39
42
45
49
rall.
ff

Dance Of The Blessed Spirits

From 'Orfeo ed Euridice'

Composed By Christoph Willibald von Gluck

pp
cresc.
mf
tr
p
rall.
dim.

Gigue

Composed By Johann Pachelbel

cresc.

Habañera

From 'Carmen'

Composed By Georges Bizet

Allegretto quasi andantino ♩ = 72

39
f
p
cresc.
mf
44
49
f
53
p
f
57
p
cresc.
f
ff

Hungarian Dance No.5 in G minor

Composed By Johannes Brahms

Vivace
33
39
poco rit.
a tempo
p dolce
45
poco rit.
a tempo
poco rit.
51
a tempo
poco rit.
a tempo
57
f passionato

sfz
f marcato
poco rit.
a tempo
p
f

Military Polonaise

Composed By Frédéric Chopin

Allegro con brio (♩ = 92)

f
ff

ff
cresc.
f
tr
rit.
cresc.
ff

53
57
ff
61
cresc.
65
f
69

73
77
ff
80
f
83
86

Norwegian Dance Op.35, No.2

Composed By Edvard Grieg

poco rit.
21
morendo
Ped.
una corda
25
Allegro (♩ = 112)
f
p
tre corde
31
f
Ped.
37
stretto
f
p
43
ff

Tempo 1
p dolce
Ped.
p sempre
poco rit.
a tempo
pp
una corda
tre corde
sempre pp
morendo
ppp

Minuet

From 'String Quartet'

Composed By Luigi Boccherini

Fine
mp
dim.
TRIO
p
dolce
mf
f
D.C. al Fine

Pas De Deux

From 'Giselle'

Composed By Adolphe Adam

mp
f

Pizzicato Polka

From 'Sylvia'

Composed By Léo Delibes

a tempo
p
cresc.
f
fz
ten.
rit.
a tempo

p
cresc.
f
fz fz
p ben sostenuto
p
mf ten.
mf ten.

Più animato
rit.
sfz
a tempo
accel.
molto cresc.
ten.
ff

Voices Of Spring

Composed By Johann Strauss

Tempo di valse (𝅗𝅥. = 64)

26
p
32
38
f
mf
p
45
52
f

58
f
66
73
f
79
tr
85
f

91
97
103
109
115

121
f
127
pp dolce
134
p
mf
141
tr
f
149
pp

rit.
A tempo

Waltz

From 'Swan Lake'

Composed By Peter Ilyich Tchaikovsky

1 2 3 4 5 6 7 8 9